Keeping The Barbarians Out: How CIOs Can Secure Their Department and Company

Tips And Techniques For CIOs To Use In Order To Secure Both Their IT Department And Their Company

"Practical, proven techniques that will show you how to help your IT department to make the department and the company more secure"

Dr. Jim Anderson

Published by:
Blue Elephant Consulting
Tampa, Florida

Printed in the United States of America

Library of Congress Control Number: 2016919566

ISBN-13: 978-1540559029
ISBN-10: 1540559025

Warning – Disclaimer

The purpose of this book is to educate and entertain. This book
does not promise or guarantee that anyone following the ideas,
tips, suggestions, techniques or strategies will be successful. The
author, publisher and distributor(s) shall have neither liability
nor responsibility to anyone with respect to any loss or damage
caused, or alleged to be caused, directly or indirectly by the
information contained in this book.

Recent Books By The Author

Product Management

- How Product Managers Can Sell More Of Their Product: Tips & Techniques For Product Managers To Better Understand How To Sell Their Product

- Product Development Lessons For Product Managers: How Product Managers Can Create Successful Products

Public Speaking

- Changing How You Speak To Overcome Your Fear Of Speaking: Change techniques that will transform a speech into a memorable event

- Delivering Excellence: How To Give Presentations That Make A Difference: Presentation techniques that will transform a speech into a memorable event

CIO Skills

- What CIOs Need To Know In Order To Successfully Manage An IT Department: Decision Making Skills That Every CIO Needs To Have In Order To Be Able To Make The Right Choices

- How CIOs Can Make Innovation Happen: Tips And Techniques For CIOs To Use In Order To Make Innovation Happen In Their IT Department

IT Manager Skills

- Building The Perfect Team: What Staffing Skills Do IT Managers Need?: Tips And Techniques That IT Managers Can Use In Order To Correctly Staff Their Teams

- Secrets Of Effective Leadership For IT Managers: Tips And Techniques That IT Managers Can Use In Order To Develop Leadership Skills

Negotiating

- Use The Power Of Arguing To Win Your Next Negotiation: How To Develop The Skill Of Effective Arguing In A Negotiation In Order To Get The Best Possible Outcome

- Learn How To Signal In Your Next Negotiation: How To Develop The Skill Of Effective Signaling In A Negotiation In Order To Get The Best Possible Outcome

Miscellaneous

- How To Heal A Broken Leg – Fast!: Understanding how to deal with a broken leg in order to start walking again quickly

- How Software Defined Networking (SDN) Is Going To Change Your World Forever: The Revolution In Network Design And How It Affects

Note: See a complete list of books by Dr. Jim Anderson at the back of this book.

Acknowledgements

Any book like this one is the result of years of real-world work experience. In my over 25 years of working for 7 different firms, I have met countless fantastic people and I've been mentored by some truly exceptional ones. Although I've probably forgotten some of the people who made me the person that I am today, here is my attempt to finally give them the recognition that they so truly deserve:

- Thomas P. Anderson
- Art Puett
- Bobbi Marshall
- Bob Boggs

Dr. Jim Anderson

This book is dedicated to my family: Lori, Maddie, Nick, and Ben. None of this would have been possible without their constant love and support.

Thanks for always believing in me and providing me with the strength to always be willing to go out there and be my best for you.

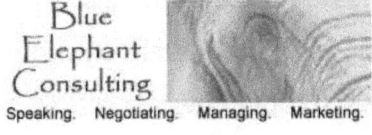

Speaking. Negotiating. Managing. Marketing.

Table Of Contents

CIOs Know That Threats Can Come From Anywhere

There are a lot of bad guys out there. For some odd reason, a lot of them seem to want to break into your company's networks and applications. As the CIO, it's your job to make sure that this does not happen. Got any thoughts on how to go about doing that?

As much as we like to spend our time looking outwards in order to detect the next threat that our company may be facing, perhaps we're looking in the wrong direction. Just as big of a deal may be the insider threat that lurks within the company. No matter where it comes from, cybercrime is your problem to deal with.

CIOs have to deal with trends as they come and go. Right now the Bring Your Own Device To Work (BYOD) phase is in full swing and if you aren't careful could cause a lot of problems for the IT department. At the same time, it's the code that your teams create that will secure your applications. Do you know if they are writing secure code or are they leaving doors wide open?

In order to measure where the threats are coming from and how big of deal they are, CIOs need to become comfortable with measuring the level of risk that they are dealing with. A big part of measuring risk is getting information about threats from other CIOs. This can be difficult to do because CIOs really don't like to share information like this.

Since we can't always be certain that we can keep the bad guys out, we need to make sure that we've taken the needed steps to secure our networks. Should they happen to get inside of the company, we need to take extra steps to make sure that they can't get what they came for. This brings up the interesting question of whether or not we should go to the effort and expense of encrypting our customer data.

No matter what our final decision on encrypting the company's digital assets is, we still have a responsibly as CIO to make sure that the company understands the threats that it is facing and that it starts to take digital security seriously.

For more information on what it takes to be a great CIO, check out my blog, The Accidental Successful CIO, at:

www.TheAccidentalSuccessfulCIO.com

Good luck!

- Dr. Jim Anderson

About The Author

I must confess that I never set out to be a CIO. When I went to school, I studied Computer Science and thought that I'd get a nice job programming and that would be that. Well, at least part of that plan worked out!

My first job was working for Boeing on their F/A-18 fighter jet program. I spent my days programming fighter jet software in assembly language and I loved it. The U.S. government decided to save some money and went looking for other countries to sell this plane to. This put me into an unfamiliar role: I started to meet with foreign military officials and I ended up having to manage groups of engineers who were working on international projects.

Time moved on and so did I. I found myself working for Siemens, the big German telecommunications company. They were making phone switches and selling them to the seven U.S. phone companies. The problem was that the switches were too complicated. Customers couldn't tell the difference between one complicated phone switch from another complicated phone switch. Once again I found myself working with the sales and marketing teams to find ways to make the great technology that the engineers had developed understandable to both internal and external customers.

I've spent over 25 years working as an senior IT professional for both big companies and startups. This has given me an opportunity to learn what it takes to manage and IT department in ways that allow it to maximize its output while becoming a valuable part of the overall company.

I now live in Tampa Florida where I spend my time managing my consulting business, Blue Elephant Consulting, teaching college courses at the University of South Florida, and traveling to work with companies like yours to share the knowledge that I have about how to create and manage successful IT departments.

I'm always available to answer questions and I can be reached at:

Dr. Jim Anderson
Blue Elephant Consulting
Email: jim@BlueElephantConsulting.com
Facebook: http://goo.gl/1TVoK
Web: **www.BlueElephantConsulting.com**

"Unforgettable communication skills that will set your ideas free..."

Create IT Departments That Are Productive And A Valuable Asset To The Rest Of The Company !

Dr. Jim Anderson is available to provide training and coaching on the topics that are the most important to people who have to manage IT departments: how can I build a productive IT department (and keep it together) while at the same time providing the rest of the company with the IT services that they need?

Dr. Anderson believes that in order to both learn and remember what he says, speakers need to laugh. Each one of his speeches is full of fun and humor so that what he says "sticks" with everyone.

Dr. Anderson's CIO Skills Training Includes:

1. How to identify and attract the right type of IT workers to your IT department.
2. How to build relationships with the company's senior management in order to get the support that you need?
3. How to stay on top of changing technology and security issues so that you never get surprised?

Dr. Jim Anderson works with over 100 customers per year. To invite Dr. Anderson to work with you, contact him at:

Phone: 813-418-6970 or
Email: jim@BlueElephantConsulting.com

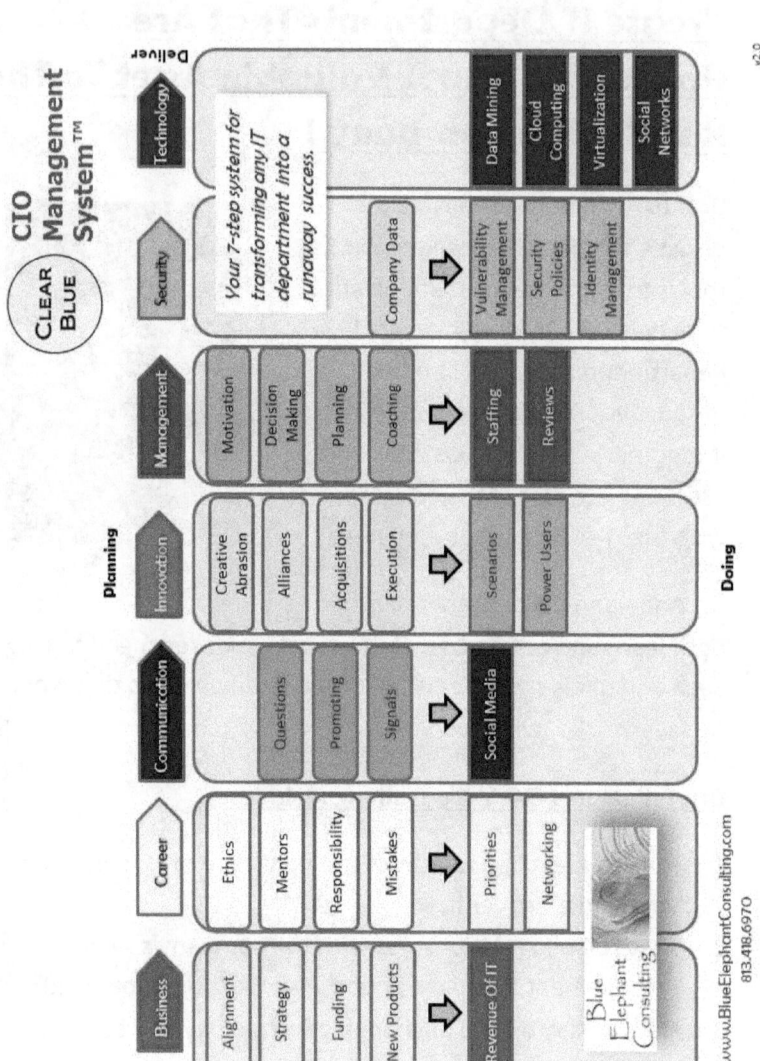

The **Clear Blue CIO Management System™** has been created to provide CIOs and senior IT managers with a clear roadmap for how to manage an IT department. This system shows CIOs what needs to be done and in what order to do it.

Chapter 1

CIO's Need To Learn How To Defend Against The Insider Threat

Chapter 1: CIO's Need To Learn How To Defend Against The Insider Threat

As a CIO you have to spend a lot of time thinking about how to protect the company's IT department. You think about hackers, viruses, Trojans, social engineering, and all of the other threats that we find in the modern definition of information technology. You buy firewalls and virus scanners and anything else that is sold to the IT sector to protect you. However, it turns out that the foe that you are trying to defend the company against may more likely be an insider. Considering the importance of information technology, **what's a CIO to do now?**

Understand What You Have To Defend

Let's face it – as CIO you are not going to be able to protect all of the company's data. What this means is that you are going to have to take the time to identify **what the really important stuff is** – that's what you're going to have to protect.

Once you've identified this, you need to take steps to make sure that it's not going to fall into the wrong hands. This can start out with **making sure that the important data is encrypted**. That's not enough. You also have to create a system to limit access to the valuable data and to keep track of just who does access it and when they touch it.

Become A Student Of Security

When you read the trade rags, you will often encounter stories that document **how thieves broke into various companies**. How clever they are never ceases to amaze me. However, the reality of real life is much different.

More often than not, when an insider decides to do something wrong they'll just be **doing the exact same thing** that someone else has done in the past. What this means for you as CIO is that once you detect someone doing something that they shouldn't, then you need to put measures in place to ensure that nobody will ever do that again.

Trust No One – Including Vendors

When we think about the insider threat that the company is facing, we often spend our time thinking about employees. However, it turns out that the number of people that we need to consider is actually much larger – **often times your vendors are almost like employees**.

What this means is that **your vendors may have access to sensitive company data**. It's what they do with this information that really matters. Since they operate both at your company as well as at your competition, you need to take steps to ensure that they don't have access to anything that you wouldn't want your competition to see.

What All Of This Means For You

Nobody ever said that the job of CIO was going to be easy, but man – they never told you that it was going to be this hard! Keeping the company safe from IT threats **could be a full time job in of itself**. It turns out that your greatest threat may not come from outside, but rather may come from the inside...

As the CIO you need to make sure that **you fully understand what assets you need protect**. You can't protect everything, so make sure that what you do protect is the most important. Take the time to learn from past attacks. If you don't, you'll be forced to repeat the learning over and over again. Finally, realize that your vendors may open a door to your IT systems that could end up costing you a great deal.

It actually is possible to keep your company secure. As CIO you need to understand that **internal threats are much more likely to cause you harm than any outside threats**. This means that inside threats are what you need to spend your time taking care of...

Chapter 2

The Threat From Within: What CIOs Need To Do To Protect The Company From The IT Department

Chapter 2: The Threat From Within: What CIOs Need To Do To Protect The Company From The IT Department

As CIO the rest of the company is **relying on you to keep them safe**. They expect you to lead the IT team in defending the corporate castle from hackers and attackers. The importance of information technology requires us to spend time doing this – it's really part of the CIO job. However, it turns out that no matter how thick you make the virtual fences that you put around the company's IT assets, you may be dealing with an even bigger threat from within your own IT department.

Who's Watching The Store?

A recent survey that was done by PriceWaterhouseCoopers revealed that 56% of the companies that responded to the survey said that they had **experienced an economic crime in the past 12 months** and the person who did it was an employee. The IT department was identified as being the #1 department that these rogue employees might be working in.

What this means to a CIO is that we need to be very, very careful **whom we invite to work in our IT departments**. Before we onboard anyone, we have some serious homework to do.

More and more firms are **conducting background checks on IT employees** that they are considering hiring. The goal of these expensive checks is to assure the rest of the company that the new IT staff can be trusted to be the ones to keep the bad guys out.

CIOs Need A Little Help From Big Brother

This, of course, leads to the next challenge for a CIO – how do you make sure that the IT staff that you have on board right now **are still honest**? Although when you hired them they were committed to helping the company to succeed, many things may have happened in their lives and some members of your IT staff may now be scheming against you.

Detecting when members of your own IT department **have switched teams on you** can be very challenging. However, voices from the field indicate that there are ways to do this.

The simplest way to detect IT staff members who may have gone rogue on you is to **keep track of when they are accessing the company's computers**. If they work a normal shift and then all of a sudden you see them logging on in the middle of the night with no clear reason as to why they are doing this, something might be up.

Another powerful way to detect when an employee has undergone a behavior change is to **monitor how they communicate**. Studies have shown that as an employee's feelings about the company that he or she works for changes, their written communication style will also change.

The types of changes that you need to be looking for include wordy people who **suddenly become very brief** in their written communication. Additionally, phrases that they use that indicate that they are angry can be another tipoff.

When you are looking for changes in an IT employee's writing style you should also look for **increased incidences of the word "me"**. When we become angry, we spend a lot more time thinking about how the world is against us and that causes us to talk about ourselves more. Finally, an IT employee who has started to plot against the company will start to reflect their more polarized way of thinking in their writing and this will show up by an increased use of words like "never" and "always".

What All Of This Means For You

If you are in the CIO position, then you have many jobs to do. One of the most important of these jobs is to **keep the company safe from people who seek to do harm to its IT systems**. No matter how well the company is protected from attacks that come from the outside, a CIO always needs to be aware that some of the most serious attacks may come from the inside.

In order to minimize the risk that an IT insider attack poses to your company, you are going to have to take steps to **prevent the problem before it starts**. This means that you are going to need to carefully screen all potential IT new hires. Once on board, you are going to have to monitor every IT employee's written communication and be on the lookout for changes in how they express themselves.

It would be nice if there was some way to **identify the good guys from the bad guys** – like if the good guys wore white hats and the bad guys wore black hats. However, things don't work that way in the real world and so CIOs have to take extra steps in order to keep the company safe. Follow these suggestions and you'll have more time to spend on the attacks that come from outside of the company.

Chapter 3

Why BYOD Spells DOOM For CIOs

Chapter 3: Why BYOD Spells DOOM For CIOs

Have you heard about the Bring Your Own Device (BYOD) craze that is sweeping companies worldwide? Employees have invested so much money along with time and effort into **customizing their smartphones, tablets, etc.** that they want to bring them to work and use them to do work. This is opening the door to a whole new world of problems for the person who has the CIO job...

What's So Wrong With BYOD?

If we spend just a moment and think back to our High School history lessons, we'll remember that **the city of Troy fell** because the bad guys brought a wooden horse that was (unknown to them) filled with good guys into their city. BYOD is sorta like that horse: your IT employees might be bringing viruses and worse into your company's IT department contained within their personal laptops, tablets, and smartphones.

Studies show that roughly 35% of mid to large size firms are allowing their employees to use their own devices while at work. This number **jumps up to 50%** when you consider smaller firms with less than 500 employees in total.

The motivation for allowing BYOD is very strong. The company stands to **save a lot of money** by not having to provide each employee with their own laptop and / or smartphone. As an added benefit, there is no learning curve when it comes to using the devices that the employees provide themselves – they already know how to use them and so the downtime associated with coming up to speed on a new device has been eliminated.

What's A CIO To Do?

Darn that coin – there's always two sides to everything! Since it looks like there are some **compelling reasons** why the company may want to take advantage of the benefits that BYOD will provide them with, what's a CIO to do?

The first step is to make sure that everyone has implemented at least the **very basic of security measures** on their personal devices. When it comes to cell phones, this means turning on password locks.

The next level of security that you'll need to implement will be to install applications that will allow you to **remotely wipe a phone or a laptop** if it gets stolen. This will remove both company information and personal information so you're going to have to be very clear with your employees: if they want to retain their personal files and photos, then they are going to have to get religion when it comes to backing up their devices that they are using at work.

As a CIO you are also going to have to wrestle with the trickiest of problems. What are you going to do about the situation where an employee who has **sensitive company information** on their personal devices decides to leave the firm and go work for one of your competitors? All of a sudden that cloud thing is starting to look a lot more attractive...

What Does All Of This Mean For You?

Since you are in the CIO position, you need to realize that there is no way to prevent the members of your IT department from bringing their personal electronics to work with them. However, it's what they are going to do with these shiny toys that a CIO needs to **step in and lay down some ground rules**. The importance of information technology is just too great to the company to allow bad things to happen because of BYOD.

The possibility of employee's personal devices **introducing a virus into the workplace** is a real problem. Also, when an employee leaves the firm, the CIO needs to make sure that they aren't taking sensitive company information with them.

All of these issues can be dealt with. The cost savings to the company of having employees provide their own IT systems is very large. However, all such benefits do **come with strings attached**. CIOs need to be very careful that BYOD does not turn into more of a problem than it's worth...

Chapter 4

Cybercrime Is The Other Guys Problem, Right CIO?

Chapter 4: Cybercrime Is The Other Guys Problem, Right CIO?

Whew! Your IT department staff who are in charge of securing the company's network have just reported to you that all patches are up-to-date and so the latest worm / trojan / virus that everyone is talking about shouldn't affect you. However, when you stop for a moment and think about **all of the companies that you do business with**, maybe it will affect you...

Why The Other Guys Really Do Matter

Just a little while ago, the headlines were full of stories about the credit card processing firm Global Payments who had suffered a massive data breech. It was estimated that this breech **compromised between 1.5M and 10M MasterCard and Visa accounts**.

These days everyone realizes that it's not just the importance of information technology, but rather the importance of the customer data that your firm stores. What makes this cyber-attack so important is who the bad guys went after. They didn't go after a bank – generally bank CIOs have done a good job of making sure that the bank's network and therefore its customer data is well protected. Instead, the crooks went after one of the bank's vendor partners and **because the bank shares customer data with them**, the cyber crooks were able to gain access to the data that they were looking for.

You may not be working in the finance industry, but the same rules apply to you: thieves may bypass your well protected network and may instead target your vendor partners whom they view as having **less stringent security measures in place**.

What A CIO Has To Do To Secure Everyone

Think for a moment about how many vendor partners your company does business with. They may not all have access to your entire customer data set, but many of them **probably have enough access that a data breech could cause you great harm**.

As the person with the CIO job you have **three different steps** that you need to take in order to ensure that your vendor partners will be able to protect your company's customer data as well as you do. The first thing is to extend the controls over customer data that your company has implemented out to your vendors. This can be as simple as ensuring that only authorized employees have access to the systems that contain the data.

The next step is to ensure that your vendors are **adequately protecting the customer data that they have**. Once again, this may be as simple as ensuring that all employee laptops use encrypted hard drives just in case they are lost or stolen. The final step is to perform periodic audits of your vendors in order to ensure that your customer data is being protected within their IT systems.

What All Of This Means For You

All too often the person who is in the CIO position focuses only on making sure that their company's networks are secure. The problem with this is that if one of your partners' IT infrastructure becomes compromised, then **your customer data may be at risk**.

CIOs need to become proactive. They need to realize that the risk of a cybercrime exists outside of their enterprise network. Both the company's data that has been shared with vendors and the company's reputation are at risk. CIOs need to partner with vendors in order to ensure that their networks are just as secure as yours are.

The benefit of working with vendors to secure their networks is that the more secure their networks become, **the less of a target that anyone with your customer data will appear to be**. In a world with so many easy targets, the cyber criminals will most likely move on to easier targets. Work with your vendors and you'll once again be able to sleep at night knowing that your customer data is secure no matter where it is.

Chapter 5

CIOs Need To Stop Their Teams From Writing Bad Code

```
* Unless the condition is true, forward
*
* This method stops the action. So, no
*
* @param   bool    $condition   A conditi
* @param   string $module       A module
* @param   string $action       An actio
*
* @throws sfStopException
*/
public function forwardUnless($condit
{
    if (!$condition)
    {
        $this->forward($module, $action)
    }
}
}
                    ...rrent request to a
                              ...ed ...
```

Chapter 5: CIOs Need To Stop Their Teams From Writing Bad Code

A big change is starting to happen in the world of IT. Just a few years ago, IT shops everywhere were busy trying to outsource just about every task that they could put their hands on. What's happened since then is that CIOs have realized importance of information technology and that **the ability to create custom code** that will allow their company to move quicker and do more is something that has to be done in-house. There's a problem however, IT shops are cranking out bad code...

The Problem With The Code That We're Writing

So what's the problem here? A software analysis company called Cast Software recently conducted a study in which they took a look at the structural quality of business application software that IT departments are producing. What they found is that the back office applications that we've always used appear to be pretty secure. However, the customer-facing applications that we've been turning out **have issues** that could cause either security problems or even outages.

The reason that our back office applications are doing ok is pretty straightforward. These applications sit on servers that are connected to few other systems. This means that **there are fewer opportunities** for software holes or gaps to show up. Generally speaking, we've had a lot of time to make these types of applications secure.

The newer applications that are being created in order to interface with customers are being written in newer languages. Unlike the COBOL language that was used to create many of the back office applications, these newer languages are still going through growing pains and **may have security holes built into them**. Additionally, a single application may have components that are written in multiple languages and this can further introduce security issues.

How To Fix The Bad Code Problem

You may be facing a situation where your IT shop is producing bad code. **What's a CIO to do?** This is a case where you are going to have to take charge. It's entirely possible that your IT team doesn't realize that they have a problem and so it's going to be up to you to educate them and show them how the problem can be fixed.

Since you have the CIO job, you need to realize that **your developers were never taught how to create secure applications**. This just isn't taught in schools. It's going to be up to you to show your teams what they need to be doing when they are writing code.

You are going to have to **set up educational programs** that will teach your developers about the common known design weaknesses that hackers use and show them how to avoid them when they are building applications. One free resource that can be used is the Common Weakness Enumeration website which provides a checklist of security holes.

Once the education process is done, **two types of analysis** need to be performed. A static analysis will allow the team to look at the entire structure of the application. A dynamic analysis will then allow them to run the code and search for performance issues.

What All Of This Means For You

As CIO you are responsible for everything that your IT department produces. That means that **the quality of the code** that your teams are producing will have your name on it. Are they doing a good job?

It turns out that recent studies have shown that a great deal of the customer facing code that is being written **has big problems**. Due to the languages that are being used, the interfaces that the software has, etc. there are major security holes in our code. If we don't take the time to learn how to write secure code, then your time in the CIO position may turn out to be very short.

The good news is that **this is a solvable problem**. By taking the time to get your IT development teams trained about what not to do, you can save yourself and your company a lot of grief. Take action today and make sure that the code that you'll be proud of is the code that they will be producing tomorrow.

Chapter 6

---

5 Things That A CIO Needs To Know About Risk

Chapter 6: 5 Things That A CIO Needs To Know About Risk

How much time every day do you spend thinking about risk? No matter what your answer was, I'm willing to bet that considering the importance of information technology **you are not spending enough time** on this important subject. Every person who has the CIO job knows that there are risks all around us each and every day. In fact, the number of risks that your company is facing is probably growing every day. The big question is what should you be doing about this?

5 Things That A CIO Needs To Know About Risk Management

When starting to think about how you want to deal with all of the risks that your company is facing, **things can become overwhelming very quickly**. What you need to do is to take the time to prioritize how you are going to be spending your time. Here are 5 things that you are going to have to know about how to most effectively tackle your risk issues:

Start With What You Know: Of course every CIO should start out by making sure that the key risk areas that the IT department is facing are covered. Key areas to be covered include making sure that your company won't experience any data breaches. Once you've got this all taken care of, it's time to look beyond the IT department. Take the time to understand how the company is using all of that data that the IT department has gathered for it and see if those other departments are exposing themselves to risk as they use what you've given them.

Don't Get Caught Up In Compliance: It can be all too easy for a CIO to become focused on a given compliance project (HIPPA,

Sarbanes-Oxley, etc.) and be left with the false sense that they've got their risk under control. These programs can help you manage your risk, but they don't do it all. What you want to do is to stay ahead of the risks that your company is going to be facing and if you are just spending your time trying to be compliant, then you're going to end up falling behind.

Look On The Bright Side: With all of the other projects that a CIO has on his or her plate, risk management may not be the one that you really want to spend much of your time working on. However, you need to realize that this type of program will provide you with an opportunity to learn more about the company's overall business processes and how it uses its IT data. Having a good understanding of this should only help to further your career.

It's All Been Done Before: The good news about setting up a risk management program for your company is that you are not the first CIO to do this. It turns out that there are a number of different "cheat sheets" that you can use to get your program off of the ground. These include ISO 31000, and ISACA's Risk-IT. However, as with all such templates, you need to keep in mind that these were not created with an understanding of your particular business' needs. You're going to have to take the time to find out how to modify them to fit the way that your company operates.

Know Who You Are Up Against: Every risk program has to be started by having you sit down and spend some time thinking about just exactly who you are trying to protect the company from. Yes, there are the usual list of external suspects. The hackers and others who are trying to get their hands on your company's most valuable secrets via social engineering or other methods. However, you also have to keep in mind that your greatest threats may be coming from your employees. These are the ones who are already on the inside and who may be able to do the most harm in the least amount of time.

What All Of This Means For You

When you are in the CIO position, you may have a more important job to do besides risk management for your company, but I wouldn't know what it would be. One of the biggest challenges that CIOs face when trying to create a risk management program is that **it can be confusing trying to determine just exactly where they should start**.

In order to get your risk management efforts off to a good start, **there are 5 things that you need to do**. You need to start the program by securing the IT department and then follow the data into other departments and make sure that they are secure also. Realize that compliance programs are good, but they are not enough. View creating a compliance program as a true career opportunity for you. Everything has been done before and that means that you can use "cheat sheets" to get your program started. Finally, make sure that you understand who you are up against so that you can create the right type of program.

Although most CIOs would rather spend their time working on programs that have to do with mobility or cloud computing, it's the risk management program that they create **that may be of the most value to their company**. Take the time to understand what you want to do and how you're going to do it and you'll be able to create a program that will keep your company's intellectual property safe and secure.

Chapter 7

CIOs Need Learn How To Defend Against The Bad Guys

Chapter 7: CIOs Need Learn How To Defend Against The Bad Guys

The person with the CIO job needs to understand that his or her company is under constant attack. Yes, some of the attacks come from hostile hackers who are always probing your company's IT defenses trying to find a way in; however, we must not forget the impact that severe weather can have on the operations of both our IT departments and our company. Clearly, **CIOs need to learn how to defend their departments and their companies against all the bad guys...**

Why Bother?

I'm going to be the first one to admit this: sometimes when we're faced with the never-ending challenge of trying to secure the company's IT resources against a threat that is not always visible, it can be very easy to just throw our hands up and say **"I give up"**. I mean, if we just put this problem on the back burner for a while would anything bad really happen? There are other bigger companies out there – won't the bad guys go after them first? Perhaps, but then there's that weather issue – it doesn't play favorites!

What this means for us is that it's really a critical part of our job to get our company ready for what might be coming down the road. If we step back for just a moment, it will become very clear to us why spending the time creating a defensive shield for our IT systems is so very important. Our companies now run on our IT systems. If they were to become unavailable because of either a hacker or weather, then most if not all of the company **would grind to a halt**. It doesn't take an accountant to figure out just how expensive that would be!

Not all risks are the same – some you need to be worrying about right now; however, **some are a bit further off in the**

future. In order to make sure that you are creating the right types of defenses that you are going to need in order to deal with your immediate problems, you are going to need to create an enterprise risk management team. Their goal will be able to help you to prioritize what defenses you should be working on now.

What Steps A CIO Can Take In Order To Be Defensive

Knowing that you need to be taking steps to create effective defenses is a great first step. However, now you need to **actually take action** in order to protect your company's IT systems. The one thing that we don't have any control over is when a hacker or severe weather is going to strike so it is our responsibility to always be ready.

Since we can't be sure exactly what kind of problems our IT department is going to be facing, **remaining agile** is one of the most important things that we can do. There are many different ways to go about doing this. The first is to take the time to prioritize your security efforts. What needs to be done now and what can be put off for a while? Additionally, you need to make your IT systems even more resilient. This means that you are going to have to prevent even minor interruptions from shutting you down.

The good news when you are faced with a task that is as large and varied as this one is that **you are not alone**. Other CIOs are facing the same challenges. In order to make sure that you are successful, you can both receive and share information with other organizations. Especially important are the Federal Bureau of Investigation (FBI), the Department of Homeland Security, and other groups related to your industry.

What All Of This Means For You

Now that you have the CIO position, you are responsible for keeping the company's IT systems **up and running**. This means that you need to find ways to guard against hackers and weather related disasters.

In order to make sure that you are always prepared, you are going to have to **adopt a strategy of being flexible**. Your adversaries will always be changing so you need to be changing also. CIOs also have to remember that one of their greatest defenses is good communication. Take the time to talk with others in the industry and you'll always know what is going on.

Given the importance of information technology, keeping your company safe and secure is **almost a full time task for CIOs**. However, if we remember to remain agile and take the time to communicate with others, then we'll be able to stay one step ahead.

Chapter 8

When It Comes To Cyber Threats, CIOs Don't Like To Share

Chapter 8: When It Comes To Cyber Threats, CIOs Don't Like To Share

By now we all know that our firms are under an almost constant set of attacks from a wide variety of outsiders because of the importance of information technology. Some of these attackers are simply children who are just fooling around with their computes and are trying to see how far they can get. However, other attackers could be organized criminals or even state sponsored hacking teams. As the person with the CIO job, it's your responsibility to protect your company from these assaults no matter where they come from. **Is it time to go outside the company in order to get some help?**

We're From The Government And We're Here To Help

So the way that this story gets started is when the U.S. Government proposed legislation that is intended to encourage the sharing of cyberthreat information between the government and companies in the private sector. On the surface, this seems like a great idea. In order for firms to make sure that they don't get surprised by hackers slipping in through their back door, they first need to fully understand what the threat is. You would think that if the government talked with everyone, then they'd be able to make sure that **everyone knew what kind of threats they were facing**.

One of the biggest questions that this new legislation brings up is simply **"who goes first?"** Both the government and business already have information on a wide variety of different cyberthreats. However, it's not quite clear who is going to open up and start sharing first. CIOs believe that it is the responsibility of the government to be proactive and start to share first.

What the government is proposing is that **firms share their cyberthreat information with the government's Department of Homeland Security**. This organization would then share the information that it had gathered with both other government agencies and private-sector information-sharing organizations.

Why CIOs May Be Cautious About Helping The Government

Although the idea of sharing cyberthreat information with the government seems like a good idea, **CIOs are right to be cautious**. Right now CIOs generally don't share too much information on this topic. Instead, they are just a bit shy and don't like to share too much.

The reasons that the person in the CIO position may not want to share cyberthreat information with the government are many. They include that this information **could place their firm out of regulatory compliance**. Yes, they'd like to share information but not if it's going to harm the company. Additionally, there is a concern that sharing the information will result in proprietary information being shared with their competition. Finally, if a company reveals that it has been attacked, there is always the possibility that they will be opening themselves up to some sort of a retaliatory attack.

There is another reason that some CIOs may be hesitant to share cyberthreat information with the government. CIOs are not convinced that the information that the government will be sharing with them **will be valuable to them** in helping to improve their company's security. An additional challenge that CIOs would face if they decided to share information with the government would be that they would have to scrub the data that they shared. All personal customer information would have to be removed. This is an added expense and yet another way that a company could have an unintended information leak.

What All Of This Means For You

Unfortunately, along with the CIO position comes the additional responsibility of **keeping your company safe** from all of the people who would like to do it electronic harm. You can't be sure how many people are trying to break into your network or what level of sophistication they have.

Instead, what you need to consider is **going outside to get some help**. The U.S. government recently stated that they would like CIOs to be more open in sharing information on attacks on their network with them. This idea does have some merit for CIOs, but it also comes with a set of risks. CIOs are going to have to determine if sharing such information could harm the company's reputation or cause it to be considered to be out of compliance.

When we try to deal with the complicated nature of the increasingly sophisticated attacks that are being launched against our networks, we need to **have as much information available to us as possible**. The U.S. government wants our information so that they can help other companies. CIOs should participate in this program; however they are going to have to very carefully plan what information they are going to share and when.

Chapter 9

Do We Really Need To Encrypt Our Customer Data?

Chapter 9: Do We Really Need To Encrypt Our Customer Data?

Guess what: there's been another hacker break in. This time it happened at the big U.S. healthcare provider Anthem. Nobody's quite sure how big of a breech it was, but initial guesses are saying that **tens of millions of customer records may have been copied by hackers**. What makes this break-in even worse is that Anthem didn't bother to encrypt the customer data that was sitting in their database. This means that the thieves got valid social security numbers that they could use for all sorts of bad things. What should the person with the Anthem CIO job have done?

The Case For Encrypting Customer Data

Somewhat amazingly, Anthem stored customer data, including social security numbers, for over 80 million of their customers **unencrypted in a database**. What was their CIO thinking? If Anthem had taken the time to scramble or encrypt the social security numbers that they were storing, then when the hackers broke in they would have been less valuable to them and less useful for them to use in bulk.

The shortcomings of Anthem's customer data storage decisions were revealed when they were hacked. It was discovered that hackers had broken in and had made off with copies of the healthcare data records for 10's of millions of Anthem's customers. It is believed that this may be **the single largest data breech that has ever been disclosed by a health-care company**. The hackers were able to gain access to Anthem's systems by using a stolen employee password to access the database where the social security numbers were being kept.

The question that the Anthem CIO has been wrestling with is trying to determine **if it is really worth it to use the importance**

of information technology to transform their corporate network into a locked down security zone? There are many different things that a company can do in order to secure its customer data. These include using random pass codes, limiting access to their databases from outside of the office, or using some form of complex math to scramble their customer data. However, all of these approaches come with their own set of drawbacks.

The Case For Not Encrypting Customer Data

Why ever would a CIO consider not encrypting customer data. The answer to that question is pretty simple, there is a cost associated with encryption. CIOs are tasked with **striking a careful balancing act** between keeping customer information secure and at the same time making it useful to the company's employees who want to use it.

If Anthem had gone ahead and encrypted its customer data, then it would have become harder for its employees to track heath care trends or share data with both state and other heath care providers. When data is encrypted, it will **slow the company's applications that access that data down**. Sometimes the slowdown will be so noticeable that the data becomes virtually unusable.

Anthem understands that it is required to maintain a customer's social security number in their system so that that member can be uniquely identified. They also understand that when the data is outside of the database, **they have to keep it secure**. That's why Anthem encrypts customer data when it moves in or out of its database. However, it is not encrypted when it is being stored in the database. Anthem uses other measures, included elevated user credentials to limit access to their customer data when it is being stored in the database.

What All Of This Means For You

What seems like a very clear case of the person in the CIO position not doing his or her job in the case of the Anthem data breech turns out to be a bit more complicated. We do know that hackers gained access to Anthem's network and then by using some sophisticated tools were able to access the health care records of tens of millions of Anthem customers. These records were stored in an unencrypted format in the Anthem database. **It's not clear if they should have been encrypted**.

Clearly, if the records had been encrypted then their value to the hackers would have been much less. However, the CIO brings up the good point that encrypting the data would **make it much harder to manage** and to exchange with other organizations that wanted to use it. Additionally, the hackers may still have been able to access it using different types of tools.

What CIOs need to understand is that their responsibility is to **ensure that their customer data is kept secure**. This means that they need to prevent hackers from being able to break into their networks in the first place. However, in the case that hackers do breach the company's walls, the CIO needs to take steps to make sure that no confidential customer data can be stolen.

Chapter 10

---

5 Things That CIOs Need To Be Doing In Order To Protect Their Networks

Chapter 10: 5 Things That CIOs Need To Be Doing In Order To Protect Their Networks

By now I think that we all realize that we are living in **dangerous and challenging times**. The bad guys know about the importance of information technology and so they spend their time trying to break into our networks and we keep trying to find ways to keep them out. You'd think that a person who has the CIO job would have to have a sophisticated set of defense measures in place in order to keep his or her network secure; however, it turns out that this is not the case. Just taking care of the basics will generally keep the bad guys out. So that brings up the question: what should CIOs be doing?

Stay Current With Patches

The software that your company uses is complex stuff. Although we'd like to think that the companies that write it have taken care to make sure that it's secure, the reality is that it's too complicated for them to have thought of everything. What this means is that there are always **"holes" being discovered in this software** that the bad guys could use to break into your company.

When the maker of the software discovers one of these holes (or is told about it by someone else), **they release a patch or an update to their software**. As a user of the software you need to apply the patch to your version of their software in order to secure it. The bad news here is that 33% of network break-ins occur because companies did not apply a patch. In fact, a study of all of the software running on computers has revealed that there are roughly 2.3 critical patches per computer that have not yet been applied. Make sure you apply patches when they become available.

Shut Your Online Doors

Every computer in your company that is connected to your network is **potentially an open door for the bad guys to walk into your network**. Having the CIO position means you need to first identify just exactly how many of these doors you have and then you need to take steps in order to ensure that they are kept firmly shut. Studies have shown that up to 25% of network break-ins were accomplished using computers that didn't have to be connected to the company's network.

The problem is that in our Internet based age, we often think that every computer and computing system that the company owns should be connected to the network. The answer is that this is not the case. Instead, only computers that require the resources that the company network can provide need to be connected. **Keep all of the other ones offline** and make sure that those doors are nailed shut.

Make Sure Important Data Is Encrypted

If the bad guys are able to get into your network, then what are they going to be looking for? **The answer is data – as much data as they can get their hands on**. The most valuable types of data will be things like payment card records, customer data, and corporate plans. All of these items have a value on the black markets.

What this means for you as CIO is that you need to do two things. The first is that you have to take a look at all of the data that your company has and **determine what data is the most valuable**. Once you've done this, you then need to implement a program to encrypt it the moment it enters your company. Yes, this will be an additional expense and it may slow things down, but the cost is well worth the peace of mind that it will provide you with.

Say Goodbye To Passwords

One of the biggest problems those of us who are trying secure networks have is that **it all relies on the end user to keep things secure**. The way that end users identify themselves to the network is through the use of a password. The problem with this scheme is that they often do a very poor job of managing their passwords.

A recent study of computer network break-ins revealed that roughly 25% of them involved the bad guys **correctly guessing a user's password**. One of the biggest problems with passwords is that we tend to use the same password on multiple systems. This means that if the bad guys break into another system and discover what our password was there, then they can use the same password to break into the company's network.

Take A Careful Look At All Of Your Vendors

In order for a company to be successful, they need to work with other companies. This is where things start to get tricky. You may do the best job in the world of securing your network. However, in order to do business with other firms, you are going to have to **permit them to access your network**. Have they secured their network?

The bad guys realize that if you've done a good job of securing your network, their best chance of getting in is to break into one of your suppliers and then **using their network to get into your network**. This is why you need to take the time to work with your vendors and make sure that they are spending as much time as you are making sure that their networks are secure also.

What All Of This Means For You

The good news is that it really is possible for a CIO to keep your network secure from the legions of bad guys who are trying to get in. However, the key to being successful in doing this is to **have a very clear understanding of just exactly what needs to be done**.

It really boils down to taking care of **the fundamental security practices** that we should all be doing anyway. These include making sure that we promptly apply patches that we receive from vendors when we get them. That we limit the number of ways that people can use to gain access to our network. That we identify what data is the most important and we encrypt it. That we stop using fallible passwords. Finally, that we take a careful look at our vendors and their security practices.

Securing your network is not hard to do. All it requires is that you **find the time to pay careful attention to the little details** that can so easily trip you up. Make sure that you have the fundamentals of network security taken care of and you will have made it so hard to break into your network that the bad guys will pick up and go elsewhere.

Chapter 11

3 Ways To Get Your Company To Take Digital Security Seriously

Chapter 11: 3 Ways To Get Your Company To Take Digital Security Seriously

As the person with the CIO job, you realize the importance of information technology and just how important it is to keep your company's network secure from all of the bad people out there in the world who are always trying to get in. You make investments in firewalls, intrusion detection devices, and highly paid IT security staff. However, we all realize that if we want to keep our network secure, we're going to need each and every employee of the company to lend a helping hand. Since in most cases they just don't seem to care about network security, **what can we do to get them to care?**

All Threats Are Personal

In order to get your company's employees to take network security seriously, you are going to have to find a way to **make this stuff "real" for them**. One great way to go about doing this is to take the time to explain to them exactly what is going on. By doing this you'll be able to make something that is as generic as "network security" very, very personal.

During your explanation you need to discuss just exactly why the bad guys are trying to break into the company's network – **what is it that they want?** Yes, some of the information that they'll be looking for will be related to company products and projects. However, a real source of gold would be all of the information that the company keeps on its employees such as date of birth, home address, and social security number. When you explain what is at risk, their motivation to participate in keeping the network safe will increase.

Help Them To Understand The Threats They Are Facing

In order for the users in your company to take the actions that are necessary to keep them and your network safe, **they need to be motivated**. What this means for you is that you're going to have to make sure that they really understand what is going on.

One way to go about making this happen is to explain to them that it may seem as though the bad guys are targeting everyone else besides your company, they really are out there and they are trying to get in. You can use security logs to make this point hit home. Additionally, when it comes time for users to apply updates, take the time to explain **why the new software will make their lives better** – not just that it's got better antivirus detection codes.

Make It Easy To Stay Safe

We all know that if we ask our end users to do too many things, take too many steps, it just is not going to happen. What this means is that we need to take steps on the IT side of the house to **make it easier** for folks to do the right thing.

This can be accomplished by **reducing the number of steps** that users have to go through in order to make updates to their computer. Additionally, since none of us like to wait for things to happen, if the changes can be downloaded in the background and be ready to be applied when we are ready, then that would speed things up significantly.

What All Of This Means For You

When you are in the CIO position, you are effectively a cheerleader for corporate network security. What this means is that not only do you have to do all of the right things, but you also have to find ways to **motivate the rest of the company** to do their part also. This is the hard part.

In order to get each employee in the company to play their role in securing the network, you need to carefully explain that the threats to the company can impact each and every one of them personally, make them understand that the bad guys **may be targeting them in particular**, and simplify the steps that employees have to go through in order to remain secure.

The good news here is that yes, it is possible to secure the company's network. However, as the CIO **you can't do this alone**. Instead, you are going to have to enlist everyone else who works at the company. You can make this happen by making the security threats that the company is facing personal and then by showing them what they need to do to keep themselves safe from the bad guys.

Chapter 12

What A CIO Needs To Know About Encryption

Chapter 12: What A CIO Needs To Know About Encryption

Due to the importance of information technology, the person with the CIO job has been handed the responsibility of **keeping the company's information assets safe**. This involves a number of different things including preventing the wrong people from gaining access to the company's networks, etc. However, there is always the possibility that company information may fall into the wrong hands, what to do when this happens? The answer is that all important information should be encrypted, but just exactly what does this mean to a CIO?

What Can A Company Use Encryption For?

Before we dive into a discussion about what your company can use encryption to accomplish, perhaps we should first take just a moment and make sure that we all have the same understanding of **just exactly what encryption is**. In a nutshell, when we are talking about encryption, we're talking about using computers to perform complex mathematical operations that turn company information into coded strings of symbols.

Every company has, by necessity, a great deal of information that it uses to conduct its business. Not all of this information is the same. Some can be classified as **being critical to the operation of the business**. This can include things such as customer information, banking information, etc. Other information is not nearly as important. Examples of this type of information include press releases, the cafeteria menu for the week, the annual list of company holidays, etc.

As the CIO you need to realize that you have two different collections of data. **It's the important data that you need to worry about the most**. You need to understand that despite your best efforts, there is the very real possibility that one day a hacker will find a way to breach the network defenses that you've put in place, By ensuring that your company's critical data is stored in an encrypted form you'll make accessing that data worthless to any hacker who might get their hands on it.

Does Encryption Really Protect A Company?

Having made a decision to encrypt your company's most critical data, as the CIO you are now going to have to start to **manage the encryption (and decryption) processes at your company**. One question that always seems to come up when we are talking about encryption has to do with the company's email: should it be encrypted. The answer is yes, but it may prove to be too difficult to do. Both the sender and the receiver would have to have access to the encryption / decryption software to make that work.

Another question that comes up as CIOs are planning how best to encrypt the company's data is trying to determine if going to the effort of encrypting it **is really going to keep the company's data secure**. The answer is a qualified yes. The encrypted data will be secure as long as the bad guys can't get their hands on the encryption keys that you are using. All too often in corporate data breeches, this is exactly what happens.

Finally, there is the somewhat obvious question of just exactly **why every piece of data at the company is not encrypted**. I mean, if you did that then you would not have to spend any time thinking about what needs to be encrypted and what you can skip. The reason that this is not a valid solution is because it takes time (even for computers) to encrypt information and so this slows everything down. Putting the systems and processes in place to encrypt and decrypt information is a difficult process. Once such a system has been set up, controlling who has access to the encryption keys then becomes yet another important task for a CIO to do correctly.

What All Of This Means For You

Let's face it, there is probably no way that any person with the CIO job can ever hope to guarantee that important company information will never fall into the wrong hands. What this means for you as the CIO is that you need to take steps before this event happens to **ensure that valuable company information doesn't leak outside the firm**. The best way to make sure your private information stays private is to encrypt it.

Encryption simply involves taking information and transforming it into unreadable information. Things that are well suited to being encrypted include customer records, anything to do with money, and company emails. In order to make sure that the bad guys can't read your encrypted information, you need to take special steps to **make sure that your encryption keys don't fall into the wrong hands**.

Encryption may not be the right answer for all company communications – the overhead may be too high in some cases. However, for the most sensitive of company information **it is probably the right choice**. As CIO you need to take the correct steps to make sure that your company's critical information is both encrypted and stays encrypted.

It's from the forge of
failure that the steel of
success is formed.

Hard Work Does Not
Guarantee Success, But
Success Does Not Happen
Without Hard Work.

- Dr. Jim Anderson

Create IT Departments That Are Productive And A Valuable Asset To The Rest Of The Company !

Dr. Jim Anderson is available to provide training and coaching on the topics that are the most important to people who have to manage IT departments: how can I build a productive IT department (and keep it together) while at the same time providing the rest of the company with the IT services that they need?

Dr. Anderson believes that in order to both learn and remember what he says, speakers need to laugh. Each one of his speeches is full of fun and humor so that what he says "sticks" with everyone.

Dr. Anderson's CIO Skills Training Includes:

1. How to identify and attract the right type of IT workers to your IT department.
2. How to build relationships with the company's senior management in order to get the support that you need?
3. How to stay on top of changing technology and security issues so that you never get surprised?

Dr. Jim Anderson works with over 100 customers per year. To invite Dr. Anderson to work with you, contact him at:

Phone: 813-418-6970 or
Email: jim@BlueElephantConsulting.com

Blue Elephant Consulting
Speaking. Negotiating. Managing. Marketi

Photo Credits:

Cover - CyberHades
https://www.flickr.com/photos/cyberhades/

Chapter 1 - Nic Taylor
https://www.flickr.com/photos/n1ct4yl0r/

Chapter 2 - Mark Fischer
https://www.flickr.com/photos/fischerfotos/

Chapter 3 - Aftab Uzzaman
https://www.flickr.com/photos/aftab/

Chapter 4 - Matt DeTurck
https://www.flickr.com/photos/dalboz17/

Chapter 5 - Thibault J.
https://www.flickr.com/photos/thibaultj/

Chapter 6 – openDemocracy
https://www.flickr.com/photos/opendemocracy/

Chapter 7 - autumnal_hedge
https://www.flickr.com/photos/autumnal_hedge/

Chapter 8 - Defence Images
https://www.flickr.com/photos/defenceimages/

Chapter 9 - Michelangelo Carrieri
https://www.flickr.com/photos/malakhkelevra/

Chapter 10 - Michael(tm) Smith
https://www.flickr.com/photos/sideshowbarker/

Chapter 11 - Phong6698
https://www.flickr.com/photos/phong6698/

Chapter 12 - Yuri Samoilov
https://www.flickr.com/photos/yusamoilov/

Other Books By
The Author

Product Management

- How Product Managers Can Sell More Of Their Product: Tips & Techniques For Product Managers To Better Understand How To Sell Their Product

- How To Create A Successful Product That Customers Will Want: Techniques For Product Managers To Boost Product Sales And Increase Customer Satisfaction

- What Product Managers Need To Know About World-Class Product Development: How Product Managers Can Create Successful Products

- How Product Managers Can Learn To Understand Their Customers: Techniques For Product Managers To Better Understand What Their Customers Really Want

- Product Management Secrets: Techniques For Product Managers To Boost Product Sales And Increase Customer Satisfaction

- Product Development Lessons For Product Managers: How Product Managers Can Create Successful Products

- Customer Lessons For Product Managers: Techniques For Product Managers To Better Understand What Their Customers Really Want

- Product Failure Lessons For Product Managers: Examples Of Products That Have Failed For Product Managers To Learn From

- Communication Skills For Product Managers: The Communication Skills That Product Managers Need To Know How To Use In Order To Have A Successful Product

- How To Have A Successful Product Manager Career: The Things That You Need To Be Doing TODAY In Order To Have A Successful Product Manager Career

- Product Manager Product Success: How to keep your product on track and make it become a success

Public Speaking

- Changing How You Speak To Overcome Your Fear Of Speaking: Change techniques that will transform a speech into a memorable event

- Delivering Excellence: How To Give Presentations That Make A Difference: Presentation techniques that will transform a speech into a memorable event

- Tools Speakers Need In Order To Give The Perfect Speech: What tools to use to create your next speech so that your message will be remembered forever!

- How To Create A Speech That Will Be Remembered

- Secrets To Organizing A Speech For Maximum Impact: How to put together a speech that will capture and hold your audience's attention

- How To Become A Better Speaker By Changing How You Speak: Change techniques that will transform a speech into a memorable event

- How To Give A Great Presentation: Presentation techniques that will transform a speech into a memorable event

- How To Rehearse In Order To Give The Perfect Speech: How to effectively rehearse your next speech to that your message be remembered forever!

- Secrets To Creating The Perfect Speech: How to create a speech that will make your message be remembered forever!

- Secrets To Organizing The Perfect Speech: How to organize the best speech of your life!

- Secrets To Planning The Perfect Speech: How to plan to give the best speech of your life

- How To Show What You Mean During A Presentation: How to use visual techniques to transform a speech into a memorable event

CIO Skills

- What CIOs Need To Know In Order To Successfully Manage An IT Department: Decision Making Skills That Every CIO Needs To Have In Order To Be Able To Make The Right Choices

- Becoming A Powerful And Effective Leader: Tips And Techniques That IT Managers Can Use In Order

To Develop Leadership Skills

- CIO Secrets For Growing Innovation: Tips And Techniques For CIOs To Use In Order To Make Innovation Happen In Their IT Department

- Your Success As A CIO Depends On How Well You Communicate: Tips And Techniques For CIOs To Use In Order To Become Better Communicators

- What CIOs Need To Know About Working With Partners: Techniques For CIOs To Use In Order To Be Able To Successfully Work With Partners

- Critical CIO Management Skills: Decision Making Skills That Every CIO Needs To Have In Order To Be Able To Make The Right Choices

- How CIOs Can Make Innovation Happen: Tips And Techniques For CIOs To Use In Order To Make Innovation Happen In Their IT Department

- CIO Communication Skills Secrets: Tips And Techniques For CIOs To Use In Order To Become Better Communicators

- Managing Your CIO Career: Steps That CIOs Have To Take In Order To Have A Long And Successful

Career

- CIO Business Skills: How CIOs can work effectively with the rest of the company!

IT Manager Skills

- Save Yourself, Save Your Job – How To Manage Your IT Career: Secrets That IT Managers Can Use In Order To Have A Successful Career

- Growing Your CIO Career: How CIOs Can Work With The Entire Company In Order To Be Successful

- How IT Managers Can Make Innovation Happen: Tips And Techniques For IT Managers To Use In Order To Make Innovation Happen In Their Teams

- Staffing Skills IT Managers Must Have: Tips And Techniques That IT Managers Can Use In Order To Correctly Staff Their Teams

- Secrets Of Effective Leadership For IT Managers: Tips And Techniques That IT Managers Can Use In Order To Develop Leadership Skills

- IT Manager Career Secrets: Tips And Techniques That IT Managers Can Use In Order To Have A

Successful Career

- IT Manager Budgeting Skills: How IT Managers Can Request, Manage, Use, And Track Their Funding

- Secrets Of Managing Budgets: What IT Managers Need To Know In Order To Understand How Their Company Uses Money

Negotiating

- Use The Power Of Arguing To Win Your Next Negotiation: How To Develop The Skill Of Effective Arguing In A Negotiation In Order To Get The Best Possible Outcome

- Learn How To Signal In Your Next Negotiation: How To Develop The Skill Of Effective Signaling In A Negotiation In Order To Get The Best Possible Outcome

- Learn The Skill Of Exploring In A Negotiation: How To Develop The Skill Of Exploring What Is Possible In A Negotiation In Order To Reach The Best Possible Deal

- Learn How To Argue In Your Next Negotiation: How To Develop The Skill Of Effective Arguing In A Negotiation In Order To Get The Best Possible

Outcome|

- How To Open Your Next Negotiation: How To Start A Negotiation In Order To Get The Best Possible Outcome

- Preparing For Your Next Negotiation: What You Need To Do BEFORE A Negotiation Starts In Order To Get The Best Possible Deal

- Learn How To Package Trades In Your Next Negotiation

- All Good Things Come To An End: How To Close A Negotiation - How To Develop The Skill Of Closing In Order To Get The Best Possible Outcome From A Negotiation

- Take No Prisoners In Your Next Negotiation: How To Start A Negotiation In Order To Get The Best Possible Outcome

Miscellaneous

- How To Heal A Broken Leg – Fast!: Understanding how to deal with a broken leg in order to start walking again quickly

- How Software Defined Networking (SDN) Is Going To Change Your World Forever: The Revolution In Network Design And How It Affects You

- The Power Of Virtualization: How It Affects Memory, Servers, and Storage: The Revolution In Creating Virtual Devices And How It Affects You

- The Internet-Enabled Successful School District Superintendent: How To Use The Internet To Boost Parental Involvement In Your Schools

- Power Distribution Unit (PDU) Secrets: What Everyone Who Works In A Data Center Needs To Know!

- Making The Jump: How To Land Your Dream Job When You Get Out Of College!

- How To Use The Internet To Create Successful Students And Involved Parents

Tips And Techniques For CIOs To Use In Order To Secure Both Their IT Department And Their Company

This book has been written with one goal in mind – to show you how you can secure both your IT department and your company. It's not easy being a CIO so we're going to show you the strategies and techniques that you can use to keep the bad guys out of your IT department!

Let's Make Your CIO Career A Success!

What You'll Find Inside:

- **CIO'S NEED TO LEARN HOW TO DEFEND AGAINST THE INSIDER THREAT**

- **WHY BYOD SPELLS DOOM FOR CIOS**

- **DO WE REALLY NEED TO ENCRYPT OUR CUSTOMER DATA?**

- **3 WAYS TO GET YOUR COMPANY TO TAKE DIGITAL SECURITY SERIOUSLY**

Dr. Jim Anderson brings his 25 years of real-world experience to this book. He's been a senior IT executive at some of the world's largest firms. He's going to show you what you need to do (and not do!) in order to make your CIO career a success!